Your Future in Cakes

The purpose of this book is to help you envision what your life will look like in the future. The running joke I've always said, is you've never seen an old pastry. While culinary chefs, cooks, and the occasional cake lady last well into their elder years, I personally haven't seen a trained pastry chef still making wedding cakes later in life.

While we all experienced the current Covid-19 pandemic and I'm sure we all took a hit in our businesses, I ran into some health issues that led to the closure of my business while still in its prime. I wasn't actively planning on closing my bakery during the holiday season of 2020 but that's exactly what happened.

After many months of physical therapy, and several check ins with the doctor (including one 2 days before I present this class), I'm eternally grateful I had a back up plan last year.

This workbook will help you shift your mindset as a business owner and hopefully give you ideas to begin implementing as a "just-in-case" policy.

I will mention a lot of ways you can diversify your income in class, if you have questions on any of them feel free to shoot my team an email: hello@studiokimihou.com

Please connect with me on social media: @chefkimihou across all platforms. I would love to invite you to check out The Baking Mama podcast, streaming on all platforms.

Let's start with a Visualization Exercise

Sit and take 3 deep breaths. Imagine it's 5 years from now. Where are you? Inside of a storefront bakery? On a television show? Teaching at conferences? On a book tour for your newest cookbook? Where are you?

- What do you smell?

- What do you hear?

Let's start with a Visualization Exercise

Sit and take 3 deep breaths. Imagine it's 5 years from now. Where are you? Inside of a storefront bakery? On a television show? Teaching at conferences? On a book tour for your newest cookbook? Where are you?

● Who do you see?

● How do you feel?

Visualization Exercise 2

Let's do that same exercise, but now it's 20 years out.

- How old are you?
- What are you doing?
- Where are you?
- What are your hobbies?
- Do you have children? How old are they?
- Did you purchase your dream home?
- Who did you mentor over the years?
- Who has mentored you?

Use this space to answer the questions on the previous page

Key Terms to Understand

Goal
A specif, desired outcome that is the object of a person's ambition or effort.

Vision
The ability to think about or plan the future with imagination or wisdom.

Dream
A cherished aspiration, ambition or ideal

Tribe
The people whom you interact with that know who you are and have a genuine interest in what you do.

Manifestation
An event, action, or object that clearly shows or embodies something, especially a theory or an abstract idea.

Grace
Courteous goodwill; a sense of propriety and consideration for others (or oneself)

Growth
The process of increasing in amount, value, or importance

Gratitude
The quality of being thankful; readiness to show appreciation for and to return kindness.

Goal Setting: *Plan to Win*

We can all relate to a social media post with "#GOALS" written in the caption. Something that we aspire to or want to achieve.

Maybe it's graduating from college, or launching a successful business, leveling up in a corporate setting, or releasing trauma from your past. Whatever the aspiration is, having a solid plan will increase the likelihood of reaching your goals.

There are three components to practical goal setting: Set your goals, create action items, and define your why. We will take a deep dive into each step and use my free goal-setting worksheet to follow along.

01 Goal Setting
"Set a goal so big that you can't achieve it until you grow into the kind of person who can." — Anonymous.

02 Creating Action Items
Goals are pure fantasy unless you have a specific plan to achieve them." — Stephen Covey.

03 Defining Your Why
"The only limit to the height of your achievements is the reach of your dreams and your willingness to work for them." — Michelle Obama.

STEP 1
Goal Setting

"Set a goal so big that you can't achieve it until you grow into the kind of person who can." — Anonymous.

Setting goals is so important because it's the gateway to the success that you dream about. When you set your goals, think about setting SMARTER goals.

You may be wondering, "I've heard of smart goals, but what's a SMARTER goal?"

Well, I'm glad you asked. SMARTER goals use the smart goals theory with an added level of accountability.

Smart Goals

SPECIFIC

Be as clear as possible when setting your goals. Drill down to the minor details because this increases your chances of reaching your goals.

MEASURABLE

Set a goal that you can measure or quantify with a metric. Earning more money isn't a quantifiable goal. Earning $5,000 in revenue is a goal you can track.

ATTAINABLE

While we encourage dreaming big and reaching for the stars, your goals should be realistic and achievable. If you're a new business owner, earning $1M in your first three months may not be attainable, but ending the quarter with profits (instead of a deficit) is attainable.

Creating *Smart Goals*

RELEVANT

Your goal should be relevant to you; it should be meaningful and impactful. Are you setting this goal because you think it will meet other people's standards? Or are you setting this goal because it aligns with your own values and beliefs?

TIME-BOUND

Setting a due date on your goals makes it easier to create action items because you have a timeline to work with.

EVALUATE

Schedule time to review your goals daily, weekly, and monthly. Ask yourself questions that keep you aligned with the goals you set. Will the work you do today help you reach those goals? Do you need to make any changes to your business costs or marketing strategy?

READJUST

After evaluating your progress against your goals, make the necessary changes to make sure you stay on track. You can do this task weekly, monthly, and quarterly.

STEP 2
Creating Action Items

After you set your goals, start breaking down your goal into smaller steps and writing down what you have to do to reach that goal. Let's use a financial goal for this example.

GOAL

Earn $5,000 per month in revenue by December 31, 2021.

Earning $5,000 per month requires making about $1,250 per week. Now think about the products you sell or the services you offer. If you sell a digital product for $29, you need to sell 44 copies of your digital product per week to earn $1,250.

If you book coaching sessions with clients for $75, you need to book 17 coaching sessions each week to meet your goal.

Take what you offer and set a weekly goal. From there, you can look at what you need to do to reach the weekly goal.

Maybe you need to strengthen your social media presence by creating more content and live videos each week. Or you may need to add a digital product and invest in Facebook and Instagram ads.

Think about the income-producing activities that you can do each week to get you to your goal of $5,000 per month.

DEFINING YOUR WHY
Step Three

"The only limit to the height of your achievements is the reach of your dreams and your willingness to work for them."
— Michelle Obama.

One of the most important (and most overlooked) parts of goal setting is defining your why. When you set a goal and attach it to a deeper meaning, you become even more motivated to reach those goals.

Why is $5,000 per month in your business important to you? Does that give you the financial freedom to leave a full-time job? Will that help you break generational poverty in your family? Do you have a dream of owning your own home someday?

What problems keep you up at night, and how can your goals help you solve them?
I challenge you to dig deep and write down YOUR why as you're setting your goals.

DREAM BIG

DREAM BIG

DREAM BIG

SEVEN
Keys to Successful Vision Planning

1 Ask yourself this question: **If I could be anything, do anything, or have anything, what would it be?** Do not focus on what you want to accomplish from afar; you need to start at the accomplishment in order to eventually tell the story how you got there.

2 .**Write down your dreams**. It's just that simple. Write. It. Down. On the pages to follow, there will be space for you to do this. Don't overthink this step! Let this part come from your innermost soul.

3 **Talk out your story**. Seriously. Imagine having the most amazing year ever and you're reflecting back on this year. What happened? This talk can be in your head, it could be with a member of your tribe, or it can be with yourself in the mirror.

4 **Categorize your list.** Create your plan, add specifics, assign due dates to various tasks, be specific, indicate if you need help, and name the people needed to help you.

SEVEN
Keys to Successful Vision Planning

5 **Create a timeline.** Remember, we know where we will end up, now it's time to map out how we will get there. Go through your list and prioritize events, people, meetings, etc. Give each item a number ranking between 1 and 5, with 1 being most important down to 5 being things that are the least important to your success. It's okay for multiple items to be assigned the same number. Continue in this fashion until everything has been assigned a number.

6 **Work at it.** In order for your goals and visions to come true, you have to do at least ONE productive thing each day by a certain time. Pick your time, e.g.: 10am to get you closer to your goal. Consistency is the key to your success. If you skip a day, make sure you double up the following day.

7 **Adapt and Overcome.** You read that right! Adapting to life as it happens is a necessary part of life. Overcoming life is what makes you stronger. Repeat these steps as often as necessary.

What are you grateful for? In life, in business, in general. List the things you're grateful for.

Dreamers Unite!
Vision planning requires Bold dreaming!

BRAINSTORM
uninterrupted. Set a timer and just day dream about what you want your life to look like. Then write it down. I do this monthly, set a schedule for what works for you and implement. Your dreams can and will change, that's okay the point is to actively dream.

OUT OF THE ORDINARY
Dream Big. What would you do if money was not a factor? Who would you actually hang out with if you had access? What would do with your spare time (if you had it).

LIVE*LAUGH*LOVE
What are you doing when you are at your happiest? What makes you laugh, who makes you laugh? What makes you love living? How do you show love? How do you receive love?

DO NOT SAY NO TO YOURSELF
As you are dreaming do not stop yourself because it feels unnatural or too hard to achieve. Do not tell yourself no. Enough people in the world will tell you no, it's your job to only say yes to yourself, your thoughts, your dreams, and your visions.

What's next for me?

Use this space to write out where you saw yourself in 5-20 years. It's time to begin planning for your next season. Will you teach? (online or in person?). Do you want to publish cookbooks? Become a ghost writer? A recipe developer? Want to work with brands? Interested in blogging? Want to start a culinary school?

What credentials do you NEED for your next season?

ACF certification? Higher Education degrees? Professional development certifications?

Who do you know that can directly or indirectly connect to your next season? Who do you need to know?

Implement the Process

P — Position yourself as an expert. Take classes or get a new certification.

R — Review your resume and update your skills. Yes, even entrepreneurs need a resume.

O — Offer a piece of your knowledge at no charge, once per quarter (Social media, in a newsletter or mentor session).

C — Categorize this workbook as a necessary step toward elevating to the next level. Come back and revisit your answers often

E — Eliminate any mental, physical, or emotional barriers to your success in your life.

S — Stimulate the economic growth by supporting other small businesses.

S — Smile and go forth in executing a plan with room for Grace, Growth and Gratitude.

GOAL SETTING: PLAN TO WIN

How to Plan to Win

What is your SMARTER goal?

PRO TIP: Use the SMARTER goals system during your goal-setting session.

"S" = Specific
"M" = Measurable
"A" = Attainable
"R" = Relevant
"T" = Time-Bound
"E" = Evaluate
"R" = Readjust

List your action items here.

Questions to ask yourself:

1. Can I make smaller weekly goals that help me reach my big goal?

2. What actions can I take each week to make progress toward my goals?

3. Are there things that you need along your journeys, such as a savings account, a website, or a planner/organizer?

Write Your Goal Here.

What's your WHY?

Now, visualize your life after you reach (and even exceed) your goals. How do you feel about your accomplishment?

Imagine what it will feel like to reach that goal. What will you do to celebrate?

"The only limit to the height of your achievements is the reach of your dreams and your willingness to work for them." — Michelle Obama

My Invitation to You

As stated at the very beginning of this book, this is to help you start thinking about a "just in case policy."

I know I was fortunate in having a backup plan after sustaining an injury that will last the remainder of my life.

Once we fully embrace the notion our Success is NOT measured by Exhaustion we will make an effort to do better.

I hope sharing my story and all of the tips I've learned along the way will inspire you to begin thinking about Life after cake. When the final order is picked up, who will you be? What will do? What would have been accomplished? What will you have leftover?

I invite you to listen to The Baking Mama Podcast, hop over to my blog ChefKimihou.com or meet me in my online academy Teach Me How To Bake for ongoing connection and support.

As always, Stay Sweet My Loves,

Chef Kimihou

MY NOTES

MY NOTES

MY NOTES

MY NOTES

MY NOTES

MY NOTES

www.ingramcontent.com/pod-product-compliance
Lightning Source LLC
Chambersburg PA
CBHW040303220526
45473CB00002B/570